AN ILLUSTRATED ACTIVITY BOOK

Wild Wonders of
MARYLAND

BY C.E. MOORE

DEDICATED TO:
BETHANY · LOLA & LUCAS
SMITH, JUNE & ELEANOR

D1479834

Wild Wonders Series
earthboundbks.com

ABOUT THIS BOOK

This book celebrates the wild things. If we take the time to look closely, we'll see that our natural world is bursting with vibrancy. The millions of interactions of minerals, seeds, and spores cause things to bloom, decay, and erode. And, if we listen closely, we might hear the creatures of these wild places — the commotion of chirps, croaks, buzzes, and hisses.

This book seeks to inspire action for a more sustainable future. When we begin to understand that we're only one part of this wonderful and weird, giant ecosystem, we will realize the costs of our actions. If we're not good caretakers of nature, we can cause major disruptions to, or worse, elimination of, other species.

This book explores biodiversity, the amazing variety of life! You'll go on a sensory journey through three remarkable wild places selected for the unique nature within them. Additional natural treasures in Maryland can be found in the sections "Water," "Plant," "Animal," and "Call of the Wild," which I hope will inspire you to learn even more about Maryland's amazing wildlife.

Come explore Maryland and be amazed by its abundance of diverse marine life in the nation's largest estuary. Venture further to learn about a remnant boreal fen, a ribbon of land rich with rare, oceanic rock, mysterious shallow depressions, and so much more!

I invite you to take a closer look at the beauty and intricacy of nature's wonders happening all around you.

C. E. Moore

Throughout this book:

- Any yellow-highlighted words can be found in the glossary on page 44.

- The conservation status of a species is an indicator of whether it still exists and how likely it is to become extinct. This book uses status rankings from NatureServe (see table below for definitions of rankings).

- There may be references to edible or medicinal plants. Never consume or pick anything you can't positively identify. Always seek an adult's guidance.

- A common name along with the genus and species names identifies each plant and animal. See "Biological Classification," page 40, to learn more.

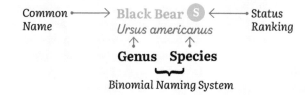

Common Name ⟶ Black Bear Ⓢ ⟵ Status Ranking
Ursus americanus
↑ ↑
Genus Species
Binomial Naming System

NATURESERVE CONSERVATION STATUS

G1 Critically Imperiled, globally
S1 Critically Imperiled, state level
At very high risk of extinction or elimination

G2 Imperiled
S2 Imperiled, state level
At high risk of extinction or elimination

G3 Vulnerable
S3 Vulnerable, state level
At moderate risk of extinction or elimination

S Secure

For a complete list of rankings, visit:
https://bit.ly/305roUQ

TABLE OF CONTENTS

MARYLAND AT A GLANCE

LOCATION

American Bison
Bison bison

Status SX: no longer in Maryland

CLIMATE

Humid Subtropical (Cfa)* and Oceanic (Cfb)*

Eastern region: typically, hot and humid summers with cold to mild winters; western region: cooler summers and longer winters.

*Köppen–Geiger climate classification system

SIX ECOREGIONS

View the map on page 5 to see where these ecoregions are located.

Basic Characteristics:

1 **Central Appalachians:** the state's highest and coldest region

2 **Ridge and Valley:** includes the majority of the state's caves

3 **Blue Ridge:** the Potomac River cuts through oak-dominated forests and valleys formed of volcanic rock

4 **Northern Piedmont:** varied landscapes of low hills, marble valleys, and vertical-walled gorges

5 **Southeastern Plains:** flat, sweeping land dotted by forests and sandy-bottomed streams

6 **Mid-Atlantic Coastal Plain:** lowest and flattest region with barrier islands and varying wetlands consisting of estuaries, salt marshes, bayous, and river deltas

Explore Further: see "Weather vs. Climate" and "Ecoregions," page 42.

During the last ice age, large beasts like bison, mastodons, and mammoths roamed through evergreen forests and across vast grasslands of what is now Maryland.

Much of Maryland's landscape some twelve thousand years ago was similar to an Alaskan tundra — cold and marshy. Some three thousand years ago, it was warm and dry. Over time, these climate fluctuations created pockets of atypical species like the bald cypress and larch trees, of which only a few stands remain in Maryland.

Geology and climate also played a role in forming Maryland's most dominant waterway, the Chesapeake Bay. As the largest estuary in the United States, it makes up a significant portion of the state's seven thousand* miles of shoreline. Biologically rich, the bay is the wintering grounds for more than one million migratory birds and supports more than 3,600 species.**

From east to west, Maryland extends 198 miles from the sandy dunes and tidal marshes of the Coastal Plain to the streams and hardwood forests of the Allegheny Mountains. With its many varied landscapes stretching across six ecoregions, Maryland embodies its popular state nickname, "America in Miniature."

Sources: *based on a 2003 Maryland Geological Survey, Maryland Department of Natural Resources; **Chesapeake Bay Program

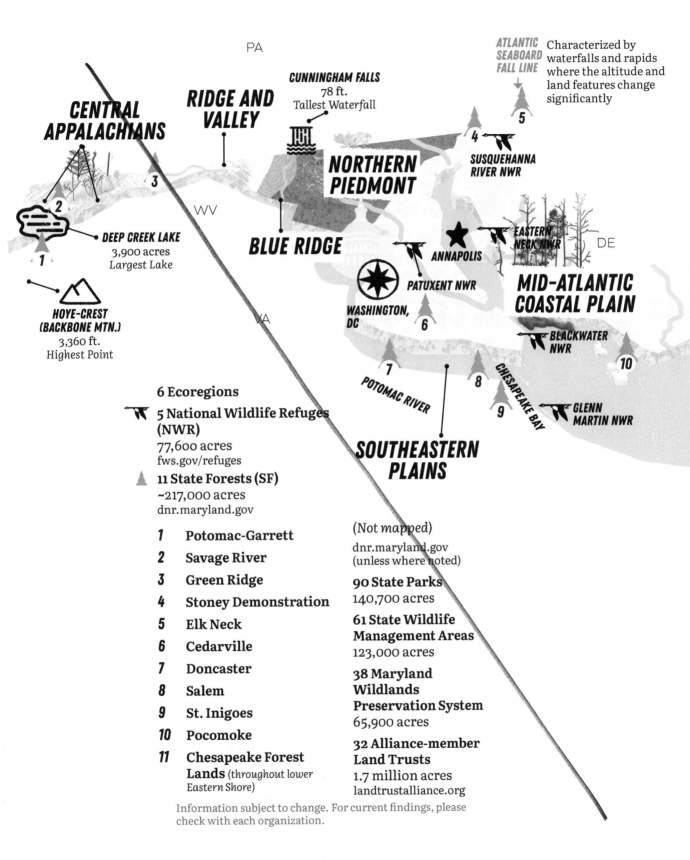

CENTRAL APPALACHIANS

RIDGE AND VALLEY

CUNNINGHAM FALLS
78 ft.
Tallest Waterfall

NORTHERN PIEDMONT

BLUE RIDGE

DEEP CREEK LAKE
3,900 acres
Largest Lake

HOYE-CREST (BACKBONE MTN.)
3,360 ft.
Highest Point

ATLANTIC SEABOARD FALL LINE

Characterized by waterfalls and rapids where the altitude and land features change significantly

SUSQUEHANNA RIVER NWR

EASTERN NECK NWR

DE

ANNAPOLIS

MID-ATLANTIC COASTAL PLAIN

PATUXENT NWR

WASHINGTON, DC

BLACKWATER NWR

POTOMAC RIVER

CHESAPEAKE BAY

GLENN MARTIN NWR

SOUTHEASTERN PLAINS

6 Ecoregions

5 National Wildlife Refuges (NWR)
77,600 acres
fws.gov/refuges

11 State Forests (SF)
~217,000 acres
dnr.maryland.gov

1	**Potomac-Garrett**
2	**Savage River**
3	**Green Ridge**
4	**Stoney Demonstration**
5	**Elk Neck**
6	**Cedarville**
7	**Doncaster**
8	**Salem**
9	**St. Inigoes**
10	**Pocomoke**
11	**Chesapeake Forest Lands** (throughout lower Eastern Shore)

(Not *mapped*)
dnr.maryland.gov
(unless where noted)

90 State Parks
140,700 acres

61 State Wildlife Management Areas
123,000 acres

38 Maryland Wildlands Preservation System
65,900 acres

32 Alliance-member Land Trusts
1.7 million acres
landtrustalliance.org

Information subject to change. For current findings, please check with each organization.

Source: Level III ecoregions defined by the Environmental Protection Agency ● epa.gov

YOUR JOURNEY

Known for your keen observation skills, you've been asked by a wildlife expert to create an exciting project that highlights Maryland's wildlife for your friends!

To get a good, general sense of the state's biodiversity, your journey will consist of two segments: *PART ONE* explores wildlife in three specific places, and *PART TWO* provides a snapshot of the flora and fauna across the state.

Along the way, you'll learn about various scientists and their work in the field (see the first one below). At journey's end, you'll have the opportunity to get creative and share your own voice about a topic of your choosing on pages 34–35.

Read below for your route and a few starter questions to think about as you embark on your wild adventure!

 1 ## FINZEL SWAMP PRESERVE

Tucked in an area between two mountains is a special atmospheric occurrence called a frost pocket where some uncommon northern species thrive.

Focus Area: The Food Web in a Peatland Habitat

- What are the benefits that peatlands provide?
- Why is it important to understand how plants and animals get their energy?

 2 ## SOLDIERS DELIGHT NATURAL ENVIRONMENT AREA

From a chromium mining site to the racing grounds of a local motorcycle club, this barren's stark landscape has had a rich, storied history.

Focus Area: Oceanic Rock and Field Observations

- How does the barren's geology influence what plants grow there?
- What kind of information can we learn by observing the natural environment?

 3 ## BLACKWATER NATIONAL WILDLIFE REFUGE

An important stopover site along the Atlantic Flyway, this refuge hosts one million waterfowl every winter, including tens of thousands of ducks and geese.

Focus Area: Birds in a Wetland Environment

- How would a tidal marsh habitat be affected by rising sea levels?
- What are ways we can describe birds?

WHO STUDIES ECOSYSTEMS? Have you ever seen a bird get nectar from a flower or an insect get caught in a spiderweb? Meet a type of scientist who studies plant and animal interactions, the kinds of relationships you'll learn about throughout this book.

 Studies how organisms interact with one another and with their physical environment.

HOW ARE ECOSYSTEMS ORGANIZED? Your neighborhood may be organized into a hierarchy: individual families make up houses, houses make up a whole neighborhood, and your neighborhood plus other area neighborhoods make up an entire town.

Similarly, ecologists also organize ecosystems from simple to increasingly complex components. Studying the ecosystem at any one level allows them to see how human actions affect the environment.

Explore Further: learn the differences between these components. See "Ecology Levels," page 40.

1
FINZEL SWAMP PRESERVE
page 8

2
SOLDIERS DELIGHT NATURAL ENVIRONMENT AREA
page 12

3
BLACKWATER NATIONAL WILDLIFE REFUGE
page 16

SUSQUEHANNA RIVER

WASHINGTON, DC

PATUXENT RIVER

POTOMAC RIVER

CHESAPEAKE BAY

ATLANTIC OCEAN

TYPES OF PLACES YOU'LL EXPLORE:

1. Boreal fen
A type of peat-forming wetland that gets the majority of its water and nutrients from a groundwater source.

2. Serpentine barren
Exposed areas with bare rock and little vegetation. Serpentine is a type of bedrock that is greenish in color due to high levels of magnesium. It dissolves easily, creating nutrient-poor soils where only certain types of plants thrive.

3. Tidal marsh
A type of wetland found along rivers, coasts, and estuaries. Tides along the Chesapeake Bay influence the rise and fall of water in the marsh.

CRANBERRY SWAMP

ESTABLISHED
1970

SIZE
326 acres

MANAGED BY
The Nature
Conservancy

CRANBERRY
SWAMP

SAVAGE
RIVER

HIGHLIGHTS

One of two remaining populations of the endangered larch in Maryland.

 Features more than 30 rare species like the alder flycatcher bird and five types of wetland habitats.

DID YOU KNOW?

Finzel Swamp is a fen, a type of peatland with a groundwater source. The water in fens causes a lack of oxygen in the soil, which means dead plant matter decomposes slowly. This gradual buildup of soil turns into peat, which takes thousands of years to form!

Peat is important because it

- stores water and nutrients to support ecosystems,
- accumulates pollen to give a snapshot of the past,
- traps carbon from decaying plant matter to reduce CO_2 in the atmosphere, and
- regulates water flow to improve water quality of nearby rivers.

Peatlands store twice as much carbon as all the world's forests!* Their protection and restoration are vital to combating climate change.

*Source: The United Nations Environment Programme (UNEP)

Explore Further: see "Classification of Wetlands," page 42.

A FEN-TASTIC TINY POCKET FOR TAMARACK

Almost 15,000 years ago, thick, massive glaciers pushed many northern plant species southward. As the ice sheets retreated, the plants moved north again except at Finzel Swamp. Species like larch, wild calla, and Canadian burnet are able to thrive in the cooler conditions created by the area's frost pocket effect. Finzel is one of the few southernmost locations in these species' range.

A SENSORY EXPLORATION

SIGHT In summer's glory, dense, whispery grasses and spotted alder thickets surround the dark, black pools of the swamp. As temperatures drop, the vivid, golden yellow of the American larch, or tamarack tree, shines bright amid the autumnal foliage.

Larix laricina S1

SMELL The remarkable eastern skunk cabbage has the ability to generate its own heat and grow through frozen ground. But hold your noses! Its scent of rotting flesh repels many animals — except bears. Hungry from their winter den, they consider this "fetid flower" a springtime treat.

Symplocarpus foetidus S

TASTE The swamp abounds in wild berry species: bright red winterberries, fleshy lobed partridgeberries, black chokeberries, sweet-tasting dewberries, highbush blueberries, and wild crimson cranberries.

TACTILE The fluffy white tuft of cotton grass acts like a sail in the wind to disperse its seeds.

Eriophorum S

SOUND The melodious rose-breasted grosbeak male has over 600 songs with which to attract mates.

Pheucticus ludovicianus S3

FINZEL SWAMP
PRESERVE

Finzel Swamp's unique combination of elevation, geographic features, and rainfall creates an interesting habitat for plants and animals competing for food.

The energy flows between organisms can be visualized through **FOOD CHAINS**.

Let's look at a possible example of a specific food chain:

fox ➡ snake ➡ shrew ➡ beetle

While this chain shows a progression of one animal eating the next, it doesn't capture the full picture of feeding relationships within the preserve.

A **FOOD WEB**, on the other hand, is a group of overlapping food chains within an ecosystem — a wider, more complex view. Just as humans change up their diet to get a variety of nutrients, many animals need to survive on more than one type of food. But an animal's next meal is always uncertain. Let's consider a scenario with the fox:

What if the owls and water snakes in a particular area eat all the mice? The fox would need another energy source. If you follow the arrows in the graphic on the right, the fox's other options are the water snake, shrews, berries, and beetles.

But there are potentially more limitations! The fox may consider only attacking smaller-sized snakes. Also, shrews expel a musky odor, which foxes often find distasteful. Shrews also have a status as an imperiled species, so there may be fewer of them for the fox to hunt. Considered an opportunistic feeder, the fox will adapt and find new nutrient sources, but other species may not be so flexible.

Studying how animals eat can provide scientists the kind of data they need to determine an area's stability.

10 **Explore Further:** see "Ecosystem Interactions," page 41.

Color the Food Web

VIDEO RESOURCE **The BrainPOP Food Chain movie:** "good for cannibals, omnivores, and vegans alike!" BrainPOP ⊕ bit.ly/35OouFv **WATCH**

PRODUCER
COTTONGRASS Ⓢ

CONSUMER
OMNIVORE
Red Fox Ⓢ
Bison bison

CONSUMER
CARNIVORE
Northern Water Snake Ⓢ
Nerodia sipedon

CONSUMER
OMNIVORE
Woodland Jumping Mouse Ⓢ
Napaeozapus insignis

CONSUMER
CARNIVORE
Northern Saw-Whet Owl **S1**
Aegolius acadicus

Because of their large size, adult beavers are less at risk to predation than kits (baby beavers).

CONSUMER
HERBIVORE
American Beaver **S**
Castor canadensis

CONSUMER
INSECTIVORE
Smoky Shrew **S2**
Sorex fumeus

CONSUMER
BEETLE

DECOMPOSER
FUNGI

PRODUCER
SKUNK CABBAGE **S**

CONSUMER
MAYFLY

CONSUMER
BLUEGILL

PRODUCER
WILD CALLA **S1**

PRODUCER
NORTHERN HIGHBUSH BLUEBERRIES **S**

11

SOLDIERS DELIGHT
NATURAL

ESTABLISHED	SIZE	MANAGED BY
1965	1,526 acres (Maryland Wildlands Preservation System)	Maryland Department of Natural Resources
	1,900 acres (designated Natural Environment Area)	

LIBERTY RESERVOIR   CHIMNEY BRANCH

LOCUST RUN

HIGHLIGHTS

Features the largest population of sandplain gerardias in the United States. This federally endangered wildflower is known to occur in only three other states: Massachusetts, New York, and Rhode Island.

Soldiers Delight is the largest remaining serpentine ecosystem in the eastern United States.

DID YOU KNOW?

Settlers called this area the Great Maryland Barrens because the landscape was stony and bare of profitable timber. The lack of some plant life is due to the presence of **serpentinite**, a beautiful **metamorphic rock** formed from the ocean's crust.

Rocks *are made of one or more minerals.* → Example: *serpentinite*

Minerals *are a collection of one or more elements.* → *Serpentine refers to a group of minerals.*

Elements *are atoms with different properties that give the rock its appearance.* → *Snakelike, with a patterned, green-black-brown coloring and slippery feel.*

SERPENTINITE is an oceanic rock formed deep within the earth where tectonic plate boundaries occur. As heat and water chemically transform the rock into its patterned appearance, it becomes lighter and essentially "floats" upward. Once exposed to the surface, it weathers to form a magnesium-rich soil. Since only certain plants can tolerate a low-nutrient environment, Soldiers Delight is a very specialized place for unique wildlife.

Learn more about serpentinite formation: U.S. Forest Service 🌐 https://bit.ly/3cQnRPr

THE SUN-LOVING SERPENTINE BARRENS

Under the open sky, a sea of little bluestem and purple three-awn prairie grasses sway to and fro across the horizon. Shrubby bear oaks, gnarled and stunted, freckle the gravelly landscape. Disrupting these neutral earth tones are the blooming colors of white asters, pink gerardias, and purplish-blue gentians. These rare beauties bask in the full warmth of the sun, attracting an array of bees and dancing butterflies.

A SENSORY EXPLORATION

SIGHT Can an ant and a caterpillar be partners? Armed with formic acid, the Allegheny mound ant escorts the Edwards' hairstreak caterpillar back and forth between the leaves of an oak's canopy and an ant-built shelter at the tree's base. In return for protection, the caterpillar secretes a sweet substance that the ant harvests, a type of relationship called mutualism.

Formica exsectoides Ⓢ

Satyrium edwardsii S1

TASTE

SOUND The coyote, or "song dog," is one of the most vocal wild mammals. Its calls come in the form of howls, whines, growls, or yips to communicate bonding or alarm, or to establish dominance.

SMELL Think you can catch a rabbit? By twitching its nose, the eastern cottontail activates 100 million receptors in its nose! And it can run 18 miles per hour hopping in a zigzag motion.

TACTILE The red-spotted orbweaver builds its silky wheel-shaped web with the use of three claws on each leg. The inner spokes allow the spider to walk freely while the outer circular threads have a sticky substance that ensnares prey. Because it eats its own web, it builds a new one each day.

Araneus cingulatus Ⓢ

SOLDIERS DELIGHT
NATURAL ENVIRONMENT AREA

Exploring wild places to understand nature's mysteries means putting our detective hats on and asking good questions about what we observe around us.

PLANT DETECTING

Identifying plants takes practice and calculated guesswork. A handy field guide of the area or a nature app can be very useful in comparing what's known (field key) and unknown (the plant). A plant detective will also need a good understanding of basic plant parts.

The flower, or corolla, is the most obvious part of some plants. Flowers have distinguishable features that make it easier to narrow down their identity. We can ask questions like:

What is the flower's size, shape, color, and symmetry? Is it long and tubular or wide and flaring? Can its plane be divided equally? What is the flower's structure? How many petals? Are the petals fused, radiating from a disc, or clustered in bunches? How are the leaves arranged? Are the leaf edges smooth or serrated? Are the veins parallel or netlike?

Scientists group plants with similar-looking properties into families. For example, species in the gentian family are typically bell-shaped and have four to five petals. Species in the aster family generally bloom late summer to fall. Learning these characteristics over time can make a plant detective's job much easier.

Match the description of each "field note" to the correct flower by placing "A," "B," "C," or "D" in the gray box.

FIELD EXPERT

BOTANIST Studies many aspects of plants and fungi.

Playing Field Detective

See blue triangles in the yellow sidebars for directions to each activity. *Answers at bottom of page 14.*

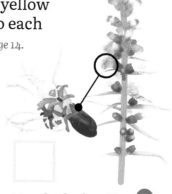

Greater Fringed Gentian **S1**
Gentianopsis crinita
Family: Gentians, Gentianaceae

Marsh Blazing Star **S1**
Liatris spicata
Family: Asters, Asteraceae

Sandplain Gerardia **G1**
Agalinis acuta
Family: Figworts, Scrophulariaceae

Serpentine Aster **S1**
Symphyotrichum depauperatum
Family: Asters, Asteraceae

Field Notes

A
- a tall spike of purplish-pink flower heads that are narrowly tubular and featherlike
- long and narrow leaves like blades of grass

Fun fact: historically used by indigenous peoples to treat swelling and abdominal pain

B
- bell-shaped flower consisting of four rounded petals with feathery edges
- leaves that are broad at the bottom and narrow into a tipping point

Fun fact: inspired many poets

C
- features 7 to 14 rays surrounding a yellow disc
- very small, tapered, and sharply pointed leaves

Fun fact: all populations occur in serpentine barrens except for one occurrence in a piedmont prairie.

D
- wide-tubed flower with pink, flared petal tips
- features sparsely grown, thin leaves

Fun fact: blossoms last only a single day.

ANIMAL DETECTING

Nature leaves many clues for us if we take the time and patience to look. Animal tracks, fur snags, eggshells, droppings, and other clues signal the presence of wildlife and their everyday happenings. These signs tell us an exciting story about what these animals have been up to!

Mud, snow, sand, and dirt provide the best opportunities to see animal tracks. We can make a best guess of who the tracks belong to with some key observations:

How many toes are there? **Hoofed mammals like elk, deer, or moose typically have two toes. Canines or felines have four toes.**

Are there claw marks? **Felines typically retract their claws when walking.**

How big are the tracks? **General knowledge of animals is helpful. Though foxes are closely related to coyotes, we know their prints are smaller. Also, bigger and heavier animals will leave deeper imprints. Seek a field guide of your area to learn typical sizes of animals.**

Are the front and rear paw prints the same? **Rabbits are a great example of animals whose front foot differs in size and shape from its rear foot.**

What kind of walker is it? **If you see more than one print, examine the spacing of tracks to see what kind of pattern the animal makes as it walks.**

Make your best guess and draw a line connecting each of the animals in the first column to its footprint in the second column.

FIELD EXPERT

WILDLIFE BIOLOGIST

Studies animals and their behavior along with the role each animal plays in its natural habitat.

Bobcat **S3**
Lynx rufus

A

3 ¾ to 5 inches long by 4 to 5 inches wide

Coyote Ⓢ
Canis latrans

B

3 to 6 inches long by 2 inches wide

Eastern Cottontail Ⓢ
Sylvilagus floridanus

C

1 ½ inches long by 1 ⅜ inches wide

White-tailed Deer Ⓢ
Odocoileus virginianus

D

2 ¼ inches long by 1 ¾ inches wide

Wild Turkey Ⓢ
Meleagris gallopavo

E

2 ½ inches long by 1 ½ inches wide

Track prints are not to scale and are based on average size of adult species. Prints are courtesy of Maryland Department of Natural Resources and Massachusetts Division of Fisheries & Wildlife.

BLACKWATER
NATIONAL WILDLIFE REFUGE

ESTABLISHED	SIZE	MANAGED BY
1933	28,894 acres	U.S. Fish and Wildlife Service

BLACKWATER RIVER

KENTUCK SWAMP

GREENBRIER SWAMP

RUSSELL SWAMP

WHITE OAK SWAMP

RACCOON CREEK MARSH

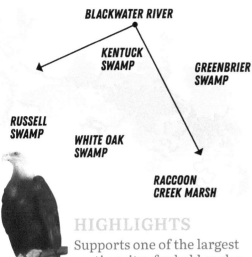

HIGHLIGHTS

Supports one of the largest nesting sites for bald eagles north of Florida and hosts the largest population of the once federally endangered Delmarva fox squirrel.

Besides 250 species of birds, the refuge also hosts 35 species of reptiles and amphibians and 165 species of endangered plants.
Source: U.S. Fish & Wildlife Service

DID YOU KNOW?

The refuge, located along Maryland's Eastern Shore, is fed by the Blackwater River and Little Blackwater River. Along with the surrounding areas of Dorchester County, this area makes up one-third of Maryland's tidal wetlands.

The Importance of Tidal Marshes

A marsh, a type of wetland dominated by grasses and tall reeds, can signal the health of a surrounding area. Not only is a marsh a rich habitat for a variety of species, but its many functions help to

- protect against storm surges,
- lessen shoreline erosion, and
- filter out pollutants.

VIDEO RESOURCE

Observe ospreys, eagles, and waterfowl through the refuge's five streaming wildlife cameras.
Friends of the Blackwater National Wildlife Refuge
🌐 bit.ly/3cFljnB

[▶] WATCH

"THE EVERGLADES OF THE NORTH"

The Atlantic Flyway is a major north-south migratory route for birds that stretches more than 3,000 miles from Canada to Florida. For the 500 species* of birds that use the flyway, Blackwater is a crucial juncture of this mass migration. It provides shelter, nesting sites, and ample food opportunities to refuel. As fall approaches, an estimated 35,000 geese and 15,000 ducks** can congregate at the refuge with some choosing to winter there all season long!

*The Audubon Society; **Friends of Blackwater National Wildlife Refuge*

A SENSORY EXPLORATION

👁 **SIGHT** With stately poise, a long-legged great blue heron stands motionless in calm, shallow waters. It visually stalks its prey, and once the prey is in sight, the heron uses its spear-like bill to strike the fish and swallow it whole.

Ardea herodias S3

SMELL Named for the musky odor used to mark their territory, muskrats are excellent swimmers and can hold their breath underwater for 15 to 20 minutes!

👅 **TASTE** The pink or white five-petaled swamp rose mallow was historically used as a medicinal tea.

Hibiscus moscheutos S

SOUND Resembling dead leaves, the tree-dwelling eastern red bat is easy to miss. It uses echolocation, a series of sound waves it sends through its mouth or nose, to locate insects. Once a wave hits an object, it produces an echo, and the chase is on!

TACTILE The Delmarva fox squirrel uses its long, fluffy tail as a blanket to wrap around itself in cold weather.

Sciurus niger cinereus S1

17

BLACKWATER
NATIONAL WILDLIFE REFUGE

Can you guess the physical feature that sets birds apart from other animals?

Birds are the only animals with feathers, lightweight appendages that primarily serve to insulate and enable flight. We can recognize the swan by its snowy-white feathers or identify a blue jay by its unique black, white, and blue plumage.

A bird's visible characteristics of color and pattern are called **FIELD MARKS** and make each bird distinct.

 Bird-watching is not so much about knowing every bird species but about exploring and observing the world around you.

Many times, a bird is too far or high to see details. But observing its size, shape, and behavior and listening to its voice are just as helpful in identifying it. The next time you see a bird, look closer and ask yourself:

 How big is the bird? How does its size or wingspan compare to other birds you're familiar with?

 What is the bird's body type? Is it slender or thick-bodied? Does it have short or long legs?

 What is the bird doing? Does it feed on the water, in a tree, or on the ground? When flying, does it glide or repeatedly flap its wings?

 What sounds does it make? Does the bird make repeated syllables? Is the song quick or unhurried?

FIELD EXPERT
ORNITHOLOGIST (or·nuh·thaa·luh·juhst) Studies all aspects of birds including bird songs, flight patterns, physical appearance, and migration patterns.

A Bird's-Eye View

Observe the shapes of the silhouettes below. Write in the space provided which group each bird on the right belongs to. Then describe the bird in your own words (think about its body type and any visible field marks).

Answers at bottom of page 18. For descriptions, there are no right or wrong answers. You can compare your notes with the ID information of each bird profile found on the Cornell Lab of Ornithology website mentioned below.

Popular Bird Groups

Birds of Prey
Hawks, eagles, and ospreys. Medium to large birds with hooked beaks and strong talons.

Owls
Birds with large rounded heads, excellent eyesight, and soft feathers that allow for silent flight.

Pelicans, Cormorants & Frigate Birds
Water birds with most species having four webbed toes.

Perching Birds
Birds with 12 tail feathers, 3 unwebbed toes in the front, and a flexible toe in the back.

Shorebirds
Aquatic birds such as sandpipers, gulls, and plovers that are often a combination of white, gray, brown, or black.

Waterfowl
Birds comprised of ducks, swans, and geese that typically have broad, flattened bills and legs suitable for swimming.

WEB RESOURCE
🌐 allaboutbirds.org The Cornell Lab of Ornithology
Look up each bird from the website's search area to learn about its behavior, food, and nesting preferences. Each profile also has a recording you can listen to. What kind of sound or call does each bird make?

VIDEO RESOURCE
How to Draw an Owl with David Sibley
Audubon Adventures 🌐 vimeo.com/403007509
Consider starting a nature journal and record your findings with sketches and notes. Tutorials like the video resource above can help you hone your drawing skills.

WATCH

ANSWERS A. birds of prey B. owls C. waterfowl D. perching birds E. pelicans, cormorants, frigates F. shorebirds

A Red-tailed Hawk **S**
Buteo jamaicensis
Family: Raptors, Accipitridae
Habitat: Open woodlands
Group:

B Great Horned Owl **S**
Bubo virginianus
Family: Horned Owls, Strigidae
Habitat: Forests
Group:

C Wood Duck **S3**
Aix sponsa
Family: Ducks, Anatidae
Habitat: Lakes and ponds
Group:

D Marsh Wren **S2**
Cistothorus palustris
Family: Wrens, Troglodytidae
Habitat: Marshes
Group:

E Brown Pelican **S1**
Pelecanus occidentalis
Family: Pelicans, Pelecanidae
Habitat: Oceans
Group:

F Laughing Gull **S1**
Leucophaeus atricilla
Family: Gulls, Laridae
Habitat: Shorelines
Group:

WATER

MAJOR WATERWAYS

16.8K MILES OF RIVER AND STREAM CHANNELS

600K ACRES OF WETLAND

DID YOU KNOW?

Maryland has only one naturally occurring lake, Laurel Oxbow Lake. The 100 lakes and reservoirs found throughout the state are all manmade from damming rivers.

STATE FISH

Rockfish S
Morone saxatilis

Family: Temperate Basses, Moronidae

Size: 18-55 inches long

THE "STRIPER"

💬 *Rockfish is a regional name given for the manner in which I hide among rocks, but you might also know me as a striped bass because of the six to nine bands found on my body. With vision similar to humans and an acute sense of smell, I'm able to catch a variety of prey such as eels, crabs, and other fish. A large percentage of my species uses the Chesapeake Bay to spawn, so I am one of the most popular fish to catch in Maryland!*

Longest River in Maryland:
Patuxent River at 115 miles

State-designated Scenic Rivers:
Anacostia • Deer Creek • Monocacy • Patuxent • Pocomoke • Potomac (Frederick and Montgomery Counties) • Severn • Wicomico-Zekiah • Youghiogheny

State-designated Wild River:
section of Youghiogheny

The Maryland General Assembly passed the Scenic and Wild Rivers Act in 1968. Go to **dnr.maryland.gov** for current findings and to learn how the Assembly defines a "scenic" and "wild" river.

MORE THAN **18** TRILLION GALLONS — THE AMOUNT OF WATER IN THE CHESAPEAKE BAY

51 BILLION GALLONS — THE AMOUNT OF WATER FROM THE 150+ RIVERS THAT FLOW INTO THE CHESAPEAKE BAY

Source: Chesapeake Bay Program 🌐 chesapeakebay.net

The Chesapeake Bay is the largest estuary in North America and the third largest in the world. It formed 10,000 years ago when melting glaciers caused sea levels to rise and flood the Susquehanna River Valley.

Its vast watershed encompasses six states and the District of Columbia, covering an astounding 64,000 square miles. With 2,700 types of plants including 80,000 acres of underwater grasses, the Chesapeake Bay supports numerous species such as the desired blue crab to the lesser-known bristle worm. But pollution continues to threaten the thousands of species who use this critical habitat for food and shelter. Efforts to restore the bay not only protect wildlife but also provide millions of residents a healthy ecosystem for recreational and economic opportunity. For instance, in a 2009 U.S. government report, the commercial seafood industry brought in 34,000 jobs and more than three billion in sales.

Source: Chesapeake Bay Foundation

WETLANDS KEY TERMS

A **wetland** is an area where water covers the soil for significant periods of time. Wetlands vary based on climate, amount of flooding, salinity, and plant and soil type. **Explore Further:** see "Classification of Wetlands," page 42.

The Chesapeake Bay has two types of wetlands:

1. *TIDAL* - a semi-enclosed area of brackish water that is influenced by tides

Scientific term: estuarine

Common name: estuary

2. *NONTIDAL* - area dominated by trees, shrubs, or grasses with low salinity

Scientific term: palustrine

Common names: marsh, swamp, bog, fen

ANIMATED RESOURCE

Estuaries: *Nature's Water Filters* • Learn how water flows through an estuary NOAA ⊕ bit.ly/38DJTBH

▶ WATCH

ECOLOGY OF A TIDAL WETLAND

Tidal wetlands are areas with constant change because of the fluctuation in water levels. Note in the graphic below how the types of plants change as you move from the upland area to open water.

- HAVRE DE GRACE, MD
- The bay is 200 miles long
- Dorchester and Somerset counties have the most wetlands acreage
- CHESAPEAKE BAY
- VIRGINIA BEACH, VA

Nontidal Wetland (Palustrine)
Tidal Wetland (Estuarine)

TYPES OF WATER
Freshwater   Brackish   Saltwater

RIVER

RIVER

ESTUARY

OCEAN

Diagram Source: Maryland Department of the Environment ⊕ mde.maryland.gov

POND

Irregular
High Tide
Low Tide

HABITAT UPLAND	HIGH MARSH	LOW MARSH	TIDAL FLAT	OPEN WATER
FLOODING rare	floods during spring tides or storms	floods regularly	usually submerged	
TYPICAL PLANTS trees, shrubs	grasses, sedges, rushes	tall grasses	aquatic plants, algae	

WATER

Chesapeake Bay Maze

A female blue crab needs help reaching the mouth of the Chesapeake Bay to release her eggs. She must have food and support along her journey, so find the best path through ALL green check marks, and beware of predators (red x's) lurking along the way!

Answer Key on page 43.

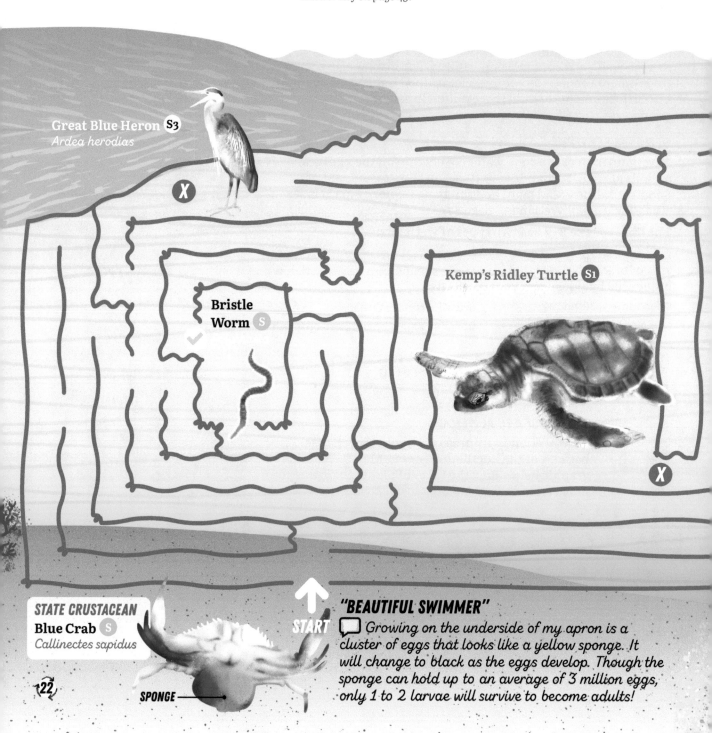

Great Blue Heron S3
Ardea herodias

Kemp's Ridley Turtle S1

Bristle Worm S

STATE CRUSTACEAN
Blue Crab S
Callinectes sapidus

START

SPONGE

"BEAUTIFUL SWIMMER"

💬 *Growing on the underside of my apron is a cluster of eggs that looks like a yellow sponge. It will change to black as the eggs develop. Though the sponge can hold up to an average of 3 million eggs, only 1 to 2 larvae will survive to become adults!*

VIDEO RESOURCE **Blue Crab 101** • Learn about the blue crab's key features and its life cycle
Chesapeake Bay Foundation 🌐 bit.ly/2O7c2uh

WATCH

FIELD EXPERT **MARINE BIOLOGIST** Studies marine organisms and their behaviors and interactions with the environment.

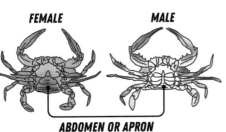

FEMALE   MALE

ABDOMEN OR APRON

WHAT'S IN A NAME?

JIMMY - an adult male with a T-shaped abdomen (called apron) and blue-tipped claws

SALLY - a juvenile female with a triangle-shaped apron

SOOK - a mature female with a round-shaped apron and red-tipped claws

SPONGE - an egg-bearing adult female

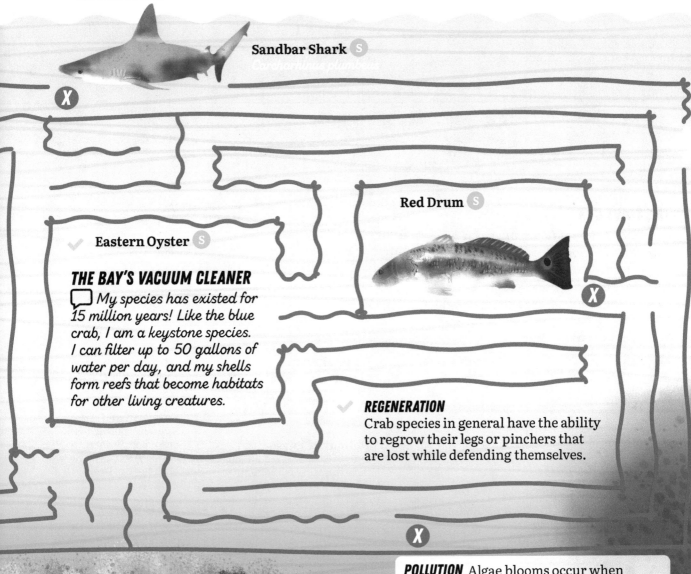

Sandbar Shark ⓢ
Carcharhinus plumbeus

Ⓧ

Red Drum ⓢ

Ⓧ

✓ **Eastern Oyster** ⓢ

THE BAY'S VACUUM CLEANER
💬 *My species has existed for 15 million years! Like the blue crab, I am a keystone species. I can filter up to 50 gallons of water per day, and my shells form reefs that become habitats for other living creatures.*

✓ **REGENERATION**
Crab species in general have the ability to regrow their legs or pinchers that are lost while defending themselves.

Ⓧ

POLLUTION Algae blooms occur when human impact, like agricultural runoff and sewage overflow, create an excess of nutrients in the water. The algae's density creates a "mahogany tide" where the water turns a brownish-red hue.

OYSTER REEF

PLANT

MARYLAND'S RARE PLANT COMMUNITIES

Below are eight examples of 59 habitats the state has identified as important for the "continued presence" of native species in their particular environment.

323
ENDANGERED OR THREATENED PLANT SPECIES

67
EXTIRPATED SPECIES

Source: Maryland Department of Natural Resources ⊕ https://bit.ly/3fDnYQa Information subject to change. Check the website for current findings.

STATE TREE
White Oak ⓢ
Quercus alba

Family: Oak or Beech, Fagaceae

Size: 80-100 feet

THE STAVE OAK

💬 *Since colonial times, my wood has been valuable for shipbuilding and home needs like furniture, flooring, and millwork. But I also play a crucial role for the hundred or so animals who consume my acorns or use my canopy to nest and roost.*

STATE FLOWER
Black-Eyed Susan ⓢ
Rudbeckia hirta

Family: Daisy, Asteraceae

Size: 1-3 feet

THE "GLORIOSA DAISY"

💬 *My cheery, golden looks are the reason so many see me as a symbol for encouragement. Along with a large dark center, I am a lovely sight to behold in early summer! But historically, I also had a functional purpose as a medicinal herb to treat various ailments like colds and earaches.*

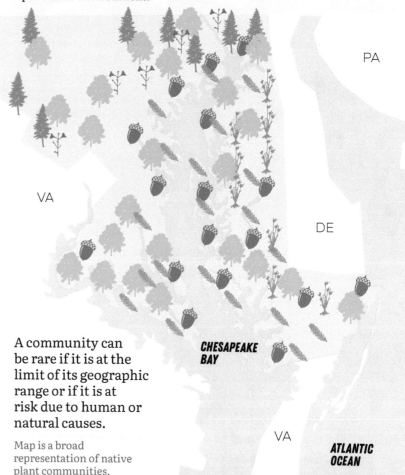

PA

VA

DE

CHESAPEAKE BAY

VA

ATLANTIC OCEAN

A community can be rare if it is at the limit of its geographic range or if it is at risk due to human or natural causes.

Map is a broad representation of native plant communities.

 Coastal Plain Oak-Pine Forest
Oak-dominated woodland that is fire-prone due to dry conditions.

 Delmarva Bays
Shallow depressions of wetland shaped by wind and erosion. See examples on page 39.

 Eastern Hemlock-Hardwood Forest
Forests occurring on mountain slopes and valleys with cool conditions.

 Mesic Mixed Hardwood Forest
Forests occurring in moist settings with nutrient-poor soils.

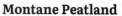 **Montane Peatland**
Highly acidic wetlands fed by a groundwater source.

 Serpentine Barren
Sparse woodlands and grassland savannas. See "Soldiers Delight Natural Environment Area," pages 12-13.

 Shale Barren
Sparse woodlands occurring in dry, steep areas prone to drought.

 Tidal Bald Cypress Swamp
Forests bordering Coastal Plain rivers featuring hardwoods and dense shrubs.

Source: Maryland Department of Natural Resources ⊕ dnr.maryland.gov

Why do we find only some species in a given area?

The infographic on page 24 shows how plant species don't occur with equal density across a geographic area. For instance, plants within the serpentine and shale barrens occur less frequently than those in a mixed hardwood forest.

Every species, whether plant or animal, has its own unique geographic range where individuals of its population live, feed, and reproduce.

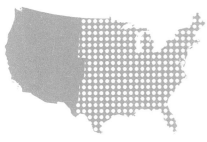

For example, this map shows how the white oak's range extends throughout much of the eastern half of the United States. Climate, elevation, soil, and access to water are just some of the limiting factors that determine where this tree can grow.

Source: U.S. Department of Agriculture 🌐 plants.usda.gov

Ways to describe population by geographic area:

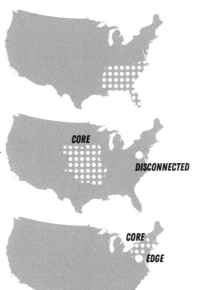

CORE POPULATIONS
Species with the highest densities occurring in a continuous geographic area.

DISCONNECTED POPULATIONS
Species that are geographically separate (disjunct) from their core populations.

CORE

DISCONNECTED

EDGE POPULATIONS
Species that occur at the edge of their natural range limits. (Maryland's latitude allows it to capture plant communities of both northern and southern floras.)

CORE

EDGE

ENDEMIC POPULATIONS
Species native to a single defined geographic location like a watershed, island, county, state, or other defined area.

MARYLAND

ENDEMIC TO THE CHESAPEAKE BAY

INTRODUCED POPULATIONS
Species that have been intentionally or accidentally brought into a region or area. Some introduced species may cause harm to their new range.

MARYLAND

EUROPE

KEY TERMS

Species Range - geographical area where a species can be found.

Population - individuals of the same species in the same habitat.

RANGE LIMITATIONS OF PLANTS

If an animal's food source becomes scarce, the animal may be able to find another location depending on its environmental needs. Plants, however, can't just pick up and move.

So, why do we find instances of isolated plant communities outside the core population?

Scientists suggest these singular occurrences were shaped by climate fluctuations over thousands of years. For instance, Maryland was at the edge of glacial activity some 11,700 years ago. Species like the larch tree favored the cooler conditions of western Maryland and remained. Then, 3,200 years ago, the climate in the region became warm and dry. Plant species you're more likely to find in the Midwest grew and prevailed.

While plants aren't as mobile as animals, they do employ various methods that can help them adapt to or expand their range.

PLANTS DISPERSE SEEDS BY:

≋ wind

🌀 **moving water** if near a river or stream

animals

· when seeds are enclosed by fruit that animals consume

· when seeds have hooks or other means to attach to fur

expulsion, with some seeds designed to eject or explode

FIELD EXPERT

BIOGEOGRAPHER Studies the migrations and areas of distribution of organisms.

PLANT

A Plant's Range

Study the maps in the plant profiles below and compare them to the **KEY** at the top of page 27 to determine if the plant's range is disconnected, edge, endemic, or introduced.

Answers at bottom of each page.

American Larch **S1**

Larix laricina

Family:
Pines, Pinaceae

HEARTY "HACKMATACK" OF THE NORTH

💬 *I'm adapted to extremely cold climates, so I mainly make my home in the northern part of the United States. Maryland is the southernmost location in my range.*

POPULATION RANGE:

Purple Loosestrife **S**

Lythrum salicaria L.

Family:
Loosestrife, Lythraceae

"MARSH MONSTER"

💬 *With the ability to produce up to three million seeds, I quickly take over any freshwater wetland. I disrupt the food chain by displacing native plants, and my thick vegetation means fewer nesting sites for birds.*

POPULATION RANGE:

Nantucket Shadbush **S1**

Amelanchier nantucketensis

Family: Rose, Rosaceae

THE JUICY "JUNEBERRY"

💬 *Typically found in New England, I was an unexpected discovery for Maryland. I'm very popular with the songbirds – my berrylike fruit is on full display by late spring.*

POPULATION RANGE:

Maryland Bur-marigold **S3**

Bidens bidentoides

Family:
Asters, Asteraceae

"ESTUARY BEGGARTICKS"

💬 *Blooming in late summer, I'm a rare species that can only be found in the freshwater tidal rivers of the Hudson, Delaware, and upper Chesapeake estuaries.*

POPULATION RANGE:

KEY

CORE
DISCONNECTED

CORE
EDGE

ENDEMIC

INTRODUCED
ABROAD

Maps of plant profiles are broad representations for illustration purposes. For more detailed information, see the U.S. Department of Agriculture Plants Database ⊕ plants.usda.gov

Bald Cypress Ⓢ
Taxodium distichum

Family:
Cypress, Cupressaceae

ANCIENT SENTINEL OF THE SOUTH

💬 *I'm a dominant feature in the sub-tropical climate of the south. But, favorable conditions in Maryland allow me to extend my range to some of the northernmost locations for my species.*

POPULATION RANGE:

Swamp Pink S2
Helonias bullata

Family:
Swamp pinks, Heloniadaceae

WONDER OF THE WETLANDS

💬 *I prefer forested wetlands with soils that aren't flooded. This may be why I'm found in small populations throughout the Atlantic coast that are isolated from each other.*

POPULATION RANGE:

Seaside Alder S3
Alnus maritima subsp. maritima

Birch, Betulaceae

AN AUTUMN BLOOMER

💬 *One of my subspecies can only be found in the swamp-like areas of the Delmarva Peninsula. Unlike other alders, I show off my golden spikes of flowers in the fall instead of the spring.*

POPULATION RANGE:

Common Chickweed Ⓢ
Stellaria media

Family: Carnations, Caryophyllaceae

"THE LAWN WEED"

💬 *With the ability to produce seeds rapidly, I have become naturalized throughout North America. Barnyard fowl are particularly fond of me, and I also have uses in herbal remedies and culinary recipes.*

POPULATION RANGE:

ANIMAL

A FEW OF MARYLAND'S RARE SPECIES

A AMPHIBIAN

B RODENT

C INVERTEBRATE

E FISH

PA

STATE BIRD
Baltimore Oriole ⓢ
Icterus galbula

Family: Blackbirds and Orioles, Icterids

Size: 6-8 inches with 9-to-12-inch wingspan

THE SWEET-BEAKED BIRD
💬 *Named after the heraldic colors of Lord Baltimore in the 1700s, the males of my species have a striking orange-and-black plumage. Favoring open woodlands and orchards, females tightly weave unique nests built from elements like grass, bark, and moss that can sit 30 feet above the ground. While I usually forage for insects high in the treetops, you could easily lure me to your backyard with a sweet offering of sugar water or fruit!*

VA

D REPLILE

DE

F CETACEAN ➡️

An animal can be rare if it has a small species population or if it occurs in a limited geographic distribution within the state.

VA

STATE REPTILE
Diamondback Terrapin ⓢ
Malaclemys terrapin

Family: Pond Turtles, Emydidae

Size: Males up to 5.5 inches and females up to 9 inches

THE SALT RESISTANT TURTLE
💬 *I may not glitter with actual diamonds, but I do have many special features. Like sea turtles, I have a unique gland that helps me filter out extra salt. I'm one of the few turtle species to live in brackish water. I also have large, webbed feet to help me swim in strong tidal currents and super strong jaws to crush crabs, snails, and other tasty marine life.*

69 LAND MAMMAL SPECIES:

OF SPECIES

	12	shrews & moles
	12	bats
	3	rabbits & hares
	22	rodents
	16	carnivores
	3	ungulates
	1	marsupial

28 MARINE MAMMAL SPECIES:

OF SPECIES

	23	cetaceans
	4	seals
	1	manatee

47 REPTILE SPECIES:

OF SPECIES

	17	turtles
	6	lizards
	24	snakes

OTHER ANIMAL SPECIES:

OF SPECIES

	20,000	invertebrates
	443	birds
	300	marine & freshwater fish
	42	amphibians

Information subject to change. For current findings, please check with the Maryland Department of Natural Resources 🌐 dnr.maryland.gov

A. Mountain Chorus Frog S1
Pseudacris brachyphona

Family: Treefrog, Hylidae   **Size:** 1-1.25 inches long

Where to find in MD: Garrett and Allegany counties

THE UPLAND CALLER

💬 My life begins in a shallow pond when I hatch from an egg as a tadpole and begin the process of metamorphosis. After a few months, I develop hind legs, and my tail grows shorter until it disappears completely. Eventually my gills are replaced by lungs to allow me to breathe outside of water where I can serenade the forest with my fast, high-pitched call.

B. North American Porcupine S3
Erethizon dorsatum

Family: New World Porcupines, Erethizontidae

Size: up to 2-3 feet in length • 8-to-10-inch tail • 11-30 pounds

Where to find in MD: Garrett, Allegany, Washington, and Frederick counties

"THE QUILL PIG"

💬 A creature of the night, I am the second largest rodent in North America after the beaver. Extending from head to tail, I have a coat of 30,000 quills featuring microscopic barbs that help me deter predators. When lodged into an attacker, the quill works its way farther into the skin making it very difficult to pull out!

C. Brook Floater S1
Alasmidonta varicosa

Family: River Mussels, Unionidae   **Size:** up to 3 inches

Where to find in MD: Allegany, Washington, Frederick, Carroll, Montgomery, and Baltimore counties

"SWOLLEN WEDGEMUSSEL"

💬 I am an important indicator of clean water because I filter out algae and bacteria. I prefer streambeds of sand and gravel in clear, flowing water. For the first few weeks of my life, I live as a parasite by attaching my larval form to a fish's gills. Once enclosed within a fish's tissue, I enjoy my host's nutrients until I reach maturity and fall off into the sediment below.

D. Rainbow Snake S1
Farancia erytrogramma

Family: Snake, Colubridae   **Size:** 3-5 feet

Where to find in MD: Montgomery and Charles counties

"THE EEL MOCCASIN"

💬 I love the water! I make my home in swamps, marshes, and slow-moving streams. Or wherever I can catch eels, the only thing I eat as an adult. I like to eat them head first! You may see my brightly colored stripes and think danger, but I am actually pretty harmless. Since I don't bite, I'll try poking my tail at a predator, but it's not pointed enough to do any harm.

E. Chesapeake Logperch S1
Percina bimaculata

Family: Perches, Percidae   **Size:** up to 4 inches

Where to find in MD: Montgomery, Harford, Cecil, and Prince George's counties

THE FORGOTTEN FISH

💬 I'm found only in the lower basin of the Susquehanna River, so little is known about me except that I can flip over rocks to find food. A naturalist identified me in 1842, but then I got misgrouped with other fish and was soon forgotten. It wasn't until 2008 that I was named a distinct species.

F. Harbor Porpoise S
Phocoena phocoena

Family: Porpoises, Phocoenidae

Size: 4-6 feet • 99-132 pounds

Where to find in MD: Calvert, Kent, Wicomico, and Worcester counties

"THE PIG FISH"

💬 I'm usually mistaken for a dolphin. Whereas they are playful and have long snouts, I'm rather shy with a short snout. This feature has earned me many names with the locals like "mere-swine" or "pig fish." My common name came about because when the fish were plentiful, I'd stay near the coast to follow them into harbor. I'm known to dive for as long as five minutes, searching for the likes of herring, pollack, squid, and other favorite snacks.

ANIMAL

Animals of Maryland Crossword

Look throughout the book to solve the "Across" and "Down" clues. Then, match the colored boxes in the puzzle to the colored fill-in-the-blanks to answer the "Who Am I?" question.

Answer Key on page 43.

ACROSS

1. The largest rodent in North America.
2. Food for blue crabs.
3. Food for adult rainbow snakes.
4. Animal whose footprint shows four toes but no claw marks.
5. Plant that is used by female Baltimore orioles to build nests.
6. A hoofed animal.
7. A color found on a male wood duck's head.
8. A red fox is this type of consumer.
9. The blue crab is known as a "beautiful _____."
10. Harbor porpoise nickname.

DOWN

1. A large beast that lived during the last ice age.
2. A type of relationship between two different species in which each benefits the other.
3. Means of using vibrations by some animals to locate prey.
4. Name of city where an oriole was named after a 1700s nobleman.
11. Substance that a diamondback terrapin can filter out of its body.
12. Defensive feature of a North American porcupine.
13. Animal who marks its territory with a musky odor.
14. The body part used by the Delmarva fox squirrel to keep itself warm.
15. An opportunistic feeder (two words).
16. A whale, dolphin, or porpoise.

WHO AM I?

I'm a federally listed endangered species found only in the Susquehanna River drainage basin of Harford County. Due to the effects of dam construction and deterioration of water quality, it is likely that I may be gone entirely (extirpated) from the state.

___ ___ ___ __Y__ ___ ___ ___ ___ ___

___ ___ ___ ___   ___ ___ ___

31

CALL OF THE WILD
CONSERVING MARYLAND'S SPECIAL PLACES

SPECIES IN MARYLAND THAT ARE GONE

129
SPECIES PRESUMED OR POSSIBLY EXTIRPATED (STATUS SX/SH) IN MARYLAND:

 67 plants   **31** insects

14 birds   **2** mussels & snails

1 reptile

2 crustaceans   **5** freshwater fishes

7 mammals including:

Maryland Darter
Microtus chrotorrhinus carolinensis

Elk
Cervus elaphus

Gray Wolf
Canis lupus

American Marten
Martes americana

Snowshoe Hare
Lepus americanus

NatureServe defines SX as "species not located despite intensive searches and virtually no likelihood of rediscovery."

STATE LISTED SPECIES IN MARYLAND THAT ARE AT RISK

476
SPECIES THAT ARE ENDANGERED, THREATENED, OR IN NEED OF CONSERVATION IN MARYLAND:

 323 plants

 153 animals

Information subject to change. For current findings, visit the Maryland Department of Natural Resources ⊕ dnr.maryland.gov

Conservation is the prevention of a wasteful use of a resource.

The Maryland Natural Heritage Program was created in 1979 to protect and restore vulnerable populations of at-risk plants and animals and their habitats. Presently, the program tracks 1,250 rare, threatened, and endangered species.

STATE INSECT
Baltimore Checkerspot **S2**
Euphydryas phaeton

Family: Brush-footed Butterflies, Nymphalidae

Size: up to 2.5-inch wingspan

THE BITTER-TASTING BUTTERFLY
💬 *You may find me flitting about in open, stream-fed meadows where host plants like milkweed, dogbane, and viburnums bloom. When I'm in caterpillar form, I feed almost exclusively on white turtlehead. Though my black wings with orange spots are pretty to look at, these bright colors advertise to birds that I am quite poisonous to them!*

Ecosystem Threats
The Baltimore checkerspot once inhabited 15 counties. Recent warming trends, the spread of invasive plants, habitat transformation from wetland to forest, and other stresses have reduced the butterfly's distribution to just 11 sites in 7 counties.

Conservation Efforts
Multiple organizations formed a super-squad of field experts and named it the Baltimore Checkerspot Recovery Team (BRCT) in 2012. Because many of the butterfly's populations are isolated and spread out, the team realized that creating new sites in addition to monitoring and research efforts were essential to the recovery plan.

How You Can Help
Volunteer, report a sighting, grow host plants like turtlehead, or host a fundraising event. See the Maryland Department of Natural Resources for partnering organizations and more ideas.

⊕ http://bit.ly/36jPInk

DELMARVA BAYS

Dotted along Maryland's Eastern Shore are pockmarked, shallow depressions called Delmarva bays. Some are wet throughout the year, while others completely dry up depending on the season.

How did they come to be?

Many theories have come to pass about how these oval-shaped basins formed. Locals once called them "whale wallows," believing that stranded whales caused the ponded water. But scientists now believe that wind and water erosion formed these cavities during the Pleistocene era 12,000 years ago!

Ecosystem threats

Delmarva bays are isolated and small with an average size of one acre. This makes it easy to use the recesses as trash dumps or to drain them for agricultural use. Land development and sea level rise are also factors in habitat loss, affecting rare plant species like featherfoil. This endangered, aquatic plant best thrives in shallow waters with beaver activity.

Why Delmarva bays are important.

Because of the variability in wetness, these ponds provide food and shelter for a diverse number of plants and animals. They also protect against storm surges and help reduce agricultural runoff from reaching major waterways.

Conservation success

One of the largest terrestrial salamanders in the United States, the tiger salamander only lives underground until it uses the ponds to mate. Recent egg counts suggest that the amphibian is making a comeback due to restoration efforts of its habitat.

Visit a Delmarva bay in Maryland:

- Andover Flatwoods Natural Area in Queen Anne's County
- Millington Natural Area in Kent County

VIDEO RESOURCE

Reviving a unique Delmarva bay
"Landowner Mark Furr and Jake McPherson of Ducks Unlimited experience an array of waterfowl after restoring wetlands on Furr's farmland."

Chesapeake Bay Program ⊕ bit.ly/3cnVJ6b

WATCH

Featherfoil (S1)
Hottonia inflata

Tiger Salamander (S2)
Ambystoma tigrinum

RUN WILD!
SELF-GUIDED ACTIVITIES

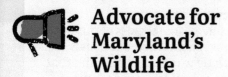 **Advocate for Maryland's Wildlife**

To advocate is to publicly support a cause.

1 Think about a story or issue from this book to use for your project.

One idea would be to create awareness for an endangered plant or animal. Questions on the right have been provided, or choose a topic of your own.

2 Choose how to execute your idea — whether it's a poster, comic strip, magazine article, or your own idea.

3 Learn more about your focus area.

For resources, go online, use local or school library resources, or talk to an expert from a local park.

4 Create your piece in the space provided on page 35.

5 Share what you know with someone else — this is how we can make positive change! Having knowledge about particular issues will help you and others to better understand how to protect Maryland's wildlife.

SPECIES NAME

_____

Describe the species' habitat.
Think about where it lives.

How does this species get its energy?
Think about where it fits in the food chain.

Describe any natural or human impacts on the species.
Are there invasive species, pollution, or impediments like dams?

What steps are being taken to protect it?

What interests you most about this species, and why do you think it's worth saving?

RUN WILD!
SELF-GUIDED ACTIVITIES

Nature Scavenger Hunt

A scavenger hunt is a great way to discover wildlife in your area. And with different approaches, the fun never has to stop! Use the ideas below to help you make a list based on your region.

Remember to respect nature — don't disturb wildlife or habitats.

- **Traditional hunt with a camera — find a physical item and take its picture:** leaf, acorn, spiderweb, bird nest, wildflowers, etc. (**Modification #1:** *see how many you can find of each item.* **Modification #2:** *create bingo cards of the items, and the first person to get all objects in a row wins.*)

- **Experiential hunt — how you experience nature:** skip a rock, touch tree bark, hear birdsong, smell a flower, etc.

MY LIST

OBSERVATIONS

Use this space to describe your hunt or sketch any observations you made. *What was interesting or difficult to find? Did you see any animal interactions?*

Design Your Own Species

As a globe-trotting adventurer, you've discovered an amazing new species! Perhaps it's an animal that is a combination between a rabbit and a lizard or a bizarre plant with fangs. Use your imagination and have fun!

1 **Record** details of its description below.

Describe its habitat.

What does it eat?

What special features does it have?

2 **Draw** your new species in its habitat using the space on the right.

SPECIES NAME

_____

RUN WILD!
SELF-GUIDED ACTIVITIES

CONSERVATION BEGINS WITH YOU!

Technology makes modern living easier for humans, and that's a good thing! But, as global citizens, we've made some choices that have disrupted and altered the environment in ways that could be irreversible.

While change in nature is inevitable, some species have specific needs for survival and may not always be able to adapt to a changing environment. Altering our behavior and taking more sustainable actions can reduce the rate of negative impact. Working together to safeguard our wild places now ensures that everyone can enjoy them in the future.

WHY WE SHOULD CARE ABOUT CONSERVATION:

We are all interconnected.
As species compete for and share resources with one another, intricate relationships emerge. Remember the blue crab? As a keystone species, it regulates the coastal marsh habitat as both predator and prey. When its numbers decline, the adverse effects result in salt grass deterioration, a vital barrier that protects the Chesapeake Bay's shorelines. Every species is linked to a multitude of others with each playing a vital role in an ecosystem.

Species extinction is happening at an accelerated rate.
Scientists are calling this time period the "age of humans"— our impact on the natural world is causing species to become extinct at an alarming rate. Perhaps there's a plant that holds the next medical breakthrough or an animal that inspires a new invention. If humans continue at our current rate, we may never find out.

LIVING A GREEN LIFESTYLE

Going green means putting into practice methods that reduce or lessen our use of natural resources. By living sustainably, we can have as little environmental impact as possible for future generations. Below is a starter list of ideas. What are some other practices you can think of?

PLAY OUTSIDE AND EXPLORE!

Practice your observation skills. Take time to really look and see the things around you. Start a nature journal to keep track of what you see. Use the questions about flowers on page 14 to hone your skills in plant recognition.

Explore this resource for journaling ideas ⊕ https://bit.ly/3jKeemS

RESPECT WILDLIFE

Admire animals from a distance, and avoid disturbing their homes. Don't pick wildflowers in vulnerable ecosystems. Practice Leave No Trace principles.

Learn more: National Park Service ⊕ https://bit.ly/3fVElF9

START A POLLINATOR GARDEN

Discuss with your family about creating a pollinator-friendly garden by planting native species.

Learn more: U.S. Forest Service ⊕ https://bit.ly/3j4XsoM

PARTICIPATE IN A COMMUNITY CLEANUP

Find and join a group near you that picks up litter from area lakes, rivers, beaches, and trails.

⊕ nationalcleanupday.org

SUPPORT ORGANIZATIONS THAT PROTECT OUR WILDLIFE

Consider raising money for, or volunteering at, a nearby nature center, local park, land trust, or wildlife agency.

Find a park: Discover the Forest ⊕ discovertheforest.org

EXPLORE FURTHER

ADDITIONAL WILD PLACES — NOTABLE MENTIONS

Assateague Island National Seashore
A 37-mile-long barrier island that hosts not only the well-known "wild" horses but also piping plovers, ghost crabs, and other species that have adapted to the harsh coastal environment.

Battle Creek Cypress Swamp Sanctuary
A nature sanctuary of bald cypress trees, one of their northernmost sites, that formed 10,000 years ago.

Masemore Hemlock Ravines Natural Area
One of the last remaining hemlock stands in Maryland's Piedmont region.

Potomac Gorge Natural Area
A dramatic landscape of terraced, rocky cliffs overlooking the Potomac River as it flows through the narrow Mather Gorge in a series of cascading waterfalls.

Sideling Hill Wildlife Management Area
Mixed oak forest featuring shale barrens formed from 300 to 400 million years ago.

EXPLORE FURTHER

BIOLOGICAL CLASSIFICATION *from page 2*

SPECIES
GENUS
FAMILY
ORDER
CLASS
PHYLUM
KINGDOM

This book focuses on these three categories.

Canines
Canidae

Gray Wolf
Canis lupus

Gray Wolf
Canis lupus

Red Fox
Vulpes vulpes

Red Wolf
Canis rufus

Red Wolf
Canis rufus

Red Wolf
Canis rufus

FIELD EXPERT

TAXONOMIST

Groups organisms into categories.

What: Taxonomists classify plants and animals based on genetics and observable physical traits like fur, gills, or feathers.

Why: Grouping species with similar makeup gives decision-makers the information they need for effective conservation planning.

Family
Just like humans, plants and animals have families, too! Each family member is different but shares enough physical similarities to be grouped together.

Genus
A group of related living things made up of one or more species.

Species
A group of similar organisms that are able to reproduce.

Scientific names are based on a set of rules accepted worldwide:

Common Name	Family	Genus	Species
Yellowhammer	Woodpecker, Picidae	*Colaptes*	*auratus*
Yellowhammer	Sparrow, Emberizidae	*Emberiza*	*citrinella*

Common names are not reliable. In this example, using the common name "yellowhammer" could refer to either the woodpecker or the sparrow.

ECOLOGY LEVELS *from page 6*

INDIVIDUAL	POPULATION	COMMUNITY	HABITAT	ECOSYSTEM
A single member of a species.	Individuals of the same species in the same habitat.	Populations of several species in one habitat.	The physical site where an individual lives, like an address for a home. Habitat surrounds a population of one species.	A community of interacting organisms (living things like plants, animals, microbes) and their environment (nonliving things like sunlight, rainfall, temperature).

Examples:

Fowler's toad	All the Fowler's toads in a given area	Fowler's toads + northern flickers + grasses in a given area	The toad's habitat could be a pond. Habitats range in size and can be as small as algae on a rock or an entire ocean.	Ecosystems can contain many habitats. The toad could live in an ecosystem including both a pond and forest habitat.

VIDEO RESOURCE

Key Ecology Terms for a breakdown of definitions · From Fuse School - Global Education
🌐 youtube.com/watch?v=E6WAQpRulhA

▶ WATCH

EXPLORE FURTHER

ECOSYSTEM INTERACTIONS *from page 10*

Ecosystems fall under two types and include both biotic and abiotic components:

TERRESTRIAL
Land-based environments like forests, grasslands, and deserts

AQUATIC
Water-based environments like lakes, ponds, rivers, oceans, and bogs

BIOTIC COMPONENTS
Parts of the Food Chain

ABIOTIC COMPONENTS
- air
- soil
- water
- sunlight
- temperature
- minerals
- nutrients
- wind

→ PRODUCERS →   **CONSUMERS →**   **DECOMPOSERS**

The sun is the ultimate source of energy on Earth.

PRODUCERS
Organisms that produce their own food. Producers create food for themselves and provide energy for the rest of the ecosystem.

CONSUMERS
Organisms that depend on other organisms for food.

DECOMPOSERS
Bacteria and fungi that break down dead organisms into organic nutrients so that plants can make more food.

> **Access to nonliving resources is limited!**

Types of Consumers

Competition

Carnivores
an organism that eats meat

Predator
an animal that lives by killing and eating other animals

Some omnivores eat some carnivores.

Omnivores
an organism that eats meat and plants

Predator and prey

Herbivores
an organism that feeds mostly on plants

Prey
an animal that is hunted and killed by another for food

Within a given area, there may be limited resources like water, nutrients, and space, so living things have to compete for these resources. They do so by:

Direct competition - Organisms interact with each other to obtain a resource
E.g., two different species who go after the same prey.

Indirect competition - Organisms affect each other's access to a resource in a secondhand way.
E.g., a change in one species' population affects another.

Ecosystem Threats
- invasive species
- climate change
- natural disasters
- disease
- pollution
- human activity

> **Resource competition is further affected by external factors.**

EXPLORE FURTHER

WEATHER VS. CLIMATE *from page 4*

WEATHER is the daily change in the atmosphere that includes conditions like temperature, precipitation, and wind. Weather lets us know what we should wear for the day!

Su   Mo   Tu   We   Th   Fr   Sa

CLIMATE is the weather of a place over a period of time. Climate looks at weather patterns that could tell us about the effects on ecosystems, crop yields, human health, and other issues at regional and global levels.

30-year span

ECOREGIONS *from page 4*

What is an ecoregion?
Earth has a variety of landforms like deserts, oceans, and mountains, but plants and animals are not distributed evenly across these landscapes. There are some types of plants you wouldn't find in a desert because their food and water needs would not be met.

Instead, both living and nonliving things reside in areas based on climate, rock formations, type of soil, and water availability — this is what is known as an **ECOREGION** (short for ecological region).

Why are ecoregions important? Similar to taxonomy, studying areas with similar characteristics gives scientists the data they need to create best practices for sustainable use of the land.

CLASSIFICATION OF WETLANDS *from pages 9 and 21*

Wetlands are defined by the plant and animal life they support, and can vary based on abiotic factors and human involvement. From the familiar names of ponds, deltas, and coral reefs to the lesser known terms of pocosins and billabongs, wetlands can be grouped into five general types of categories:

Based on the Cowardin classification system developed by the U.S. Fish & Wildlife Service

1 TIDAL — ESTUARINE
2 NONTIDAL — PALUSTRINE
3 LAKES & RESERVOIRS — LACUSTRINE
4 RIVERS — RIVERINE
5 OPEN OCEAN — MARINE

Nontidal wetlands can be grouped into four main habitat types:

	Bog	Fen	Marsh	Swamp
FEATURES	peat-forming wetland with main water source from precipitation	peat-forming wetland with main water source from groundwater	low-lying wetland frequently filled with water; can also be tidal	wetland dominated by trees and shrubs that are adapted to water
SOIL	highly acidic, nutrient-poor soil	flowing water source provides more nutrients than bogs	nutrient-rich	nutrients of soil dependent upon type of swamp
SAMPLE WILDLIFE	sphagnum moss, carnivorous plants, beavers, salamanders, and more	wildflowers, deer, grasses, turtles, fish, and more	grasses, sedges, rushes, muskrats, various birds, and more	cypress, cattails, swamp lilies, frogs, raccoons, snakes, and more

ANSWER KEY

PAGES 22-23: CHESAPEAKE BAY MAZE

PAGES 30-31: ANIMALS OF MARYLAND CROSSWORD

Across/Down entries:

1 BEAVER
2 MUSSELS
3 EELS
4 BOBCAT
5 MOSS
6 UNGULATE
7 GREEN
8 OMNIVORE
9 SWIMMER
10 MERESWINE
11 SALT
12 QUILL
13 MUSKRAT
14 TAIL
15 RED FOX
16 CETACEA

BION / MUTUALISM / ECHOLOCATE / BALTIMORE / RED / OMNIVORE

WHO AM I?

M A R Y L A N D

D A R T E R

GLOSSARY

abiotic · *noun*
A nonliving thing.

appendage · *noun*
A limb or other body part attached to the main trunk of the body.

bayou · *noun*
A body of water (as a creek) that flows slowly through marshy land.

biodiversity · *noun*
The variety of life in the world or in a particular habitat or ecosystem.

biotic · *noun*
A living thing.

boreal · *adjective*
Of, relating to, or located in northern regions.

brackish water · *noun*
Salt water and fresh water mixed together.

carnivore · *noun*
(Of an animal) an organism that eats mostly meat, or the flesh of animals.

(Of a plant) an organism that traps and digests small animals, especially insects.

cetacean · *noun*
A whale, dolphin, or porpoise.

conservation · *noun*
Prevention of wasteful use of a resource.

corolla · *noun*
The petals of a flower.

delta · *noun*
A piece of land in the shape of a triangle or fan made by deposits of mud and sand at the mouth of a river.

ecosystem · *noun*
Includes all of the living things (plants, animals, and organisms) in a given area, interacting with each other and also with their nonliving environments (weather, earth, sun, soil, climate, atmosphere).

endemic · *adjective*
When a native plant or animal is restricted to a certain place.

environment · *noun*
All of the biotic and abiotic factors that act on an organism, population, or ecological community and influence its survival and development.

estuary · *noun*
An area where seawater mixes with fresh water.

extirpated species · *noun*
A species or population that no longer exists within a certain geographical location.

fauna · *noun*
The animals of a particular region, habitat, or geological period.

flora · *noun*
The plants of a particular region, habitat, or geological period.

food chain · *noun*
The flow of energy and nutrients from one organism to another.

formic acid · *noun*
A colorless, caustic, fuming liquid that occurs naturally as the poison of ants and stinging nettles.

frost pocket · *noun*
A low-lying area where cool air accumulates.

habitat · *noun*
Physical location of a community, population, and individuals.

herbivore · *noun*
An organism that feeds mostly on plants.

insectivore · *noun*
An organism that feeds mostly on insects.

invasive species · *noun*
Organisms that are nonnative (or alien) in a given region and whose introduction is likely to have a negative effect.

keystone species · *noun*
A species on which other species in an ecosystem largely depend, such that if it were removed, the ecosystem would change drastically.

mammal · *noun*
An animal that breathes air, has a backbone, and grows hair at some point during its life. Female mammals have glands that can produce milk.

mesic · *adjective*
When an environment or habitat contains a moderate amount of moisture.

metamorphic rock · *noun*
Rock that was once one form of rock but has changed to another under the influence of heat, pressure, and hot mineral-rich fluids.

metamorphosis · *noun*
The physical change that occurs when an insect or amphibian transforms from an immature form to an adult form in two or more distinct stages.

montane · *adjective*
Of or inhabiting mountainous country.

mutualism · *noun*
An interaction between organisms of two different species in which each benefits.

opportunistic feeder · *noun*
An organism that can thrive on any available nutrient source.

organism · *noun*
A living thing such as an animal, plant, or microorganism capable of reproduction, growth, and maintenance.

omnivore · *noun*
An organism that regularly consumes plants, animals, algae, and fungi.

peat · *noun*
Decaying plant matter typically found in wetlands like bogs and swamps.

salinity · *noun*
The concentration of dissolved salt in a given volume of water.

serpentinite · *noun*
A dark, typically greenish metamorphic rock consisting largely of serpentine or related minerals, formed when igneous rocks are altered by water.

sustainability · *noun*
Avoidance of the depletion of natural resources in order to maintain an ecological balance.

ungulate · *noun*
A hoofed mammal.

watershed · *noun*
An area of land where all water drains to a central point like a lake, river, or stream.

CPSIA information can be obtained
at www.ICGtesting.com
Printed in the USA
LVHW072049150521
687550LV00002B/4